MENTAL POISONING

▽ ▽ ▽

Mental Poisoning

BY

H. SPENCER LEWIS, Ph.D.

Author of

"Mansions of the Soul," "The Symbolic
Prophecy of the Great Pyramid," "A
Thousand Years of Yesterdays," "Self
Mastery and Fate," etc.

ROSICRUCIAN LIBRARY
VOLUME XVII

SUPREME GRAND LODGE OF AMORC
Printing and Publishing Department
San Jose, California

First Edition................1937
Second Edition...............1942
Third Edition................1947
Fourth Edition...............1951

THE ROSICRUCIAN PRESS, LTD.
San Jose, California

FIFTH EDITION...............1956

PANTAGRAPH PRINTING AND STATIONERY COMPANY
Bloomington, Illinois

SIXTH EDITION...............1959

Printed and Bound in the United States of America
Kingsport Press, Inc., Kingsport, Tenn.

DEDICATION

▽

To the thousands of unfortunate men and
women who have fallen prey to the
poisoned darts of subtle, sordid,
destructive suggestions. May this
work be the means of making
thousands of other humans
immune to this noxious
influence.

▽

The Rosicrucian Library

▽   ▽   ▽

*(Other volumes will be added from time to time.
Write for complete catalogue.)*

CONTENTS

▽

▽   ▽   ▽

The above is the view of the famous temple tomb of Queen Hatshepsut, 1500 B.C., filmed by the AMORC camera expedition. In this mysterious, rugged Valley of the Nile, surrounded by walls of sandstone, are buried Egypt's great, the Pharaohs and kings of the past. Most of these temple tombs carry inscriptions of warning to all those who would dare to invade their sanctity, threatening dire consequences to the desecrater.

Portion of the famous Rameseum, the tomb-temple built by Rameses II in the Nineteenth Dynasty at Thebes. The colossal figures are of Rameses, a gesture of vanity. The ancient rites practised in this sanctuary were often misunderstood by the awe-inspired laymen and became the foundation for superstitions which persisted for centuries. (Filmed by the AMORC Camera Expedition)

The above view is of a sarcophagus chamber (mummy room) of the recently excavated pyramid temple. This little temple is near the Sphinx and some little distance from the base of the pyramid, and was originally connected by a long causeway or ramp, in which ceremonies for the departed were held. Later, further ceremonies and initiations were held in the Great Pyramid itself. In such temples as these, attempts were made by the learned to overcome the superstitions and fears, the mental poisoning of the day.

Note the Egyptian fellah in the middle distance of the above view, making his salutation to the past in the giant hypostyle of the Temple. Also observe the deeply engraved hieroglyphs on the columns. To the illiterate and uneducated, these hieroglyphs were evil designs which cast fear into their hearts. The mental poisoning which it caused them was due to their ignorance and superstition, rather than to any intent on the part of the priesthood, scribes or Pharaohs.

HYPNOTISM OR BLACK MAGIC?

HE strange deaths that came to so large a number of the explorers taking part in the excavations of King Tut's tomb gradually awakened throughout the entire world an interest in the ancient beliefs in black magic and magical curses.

The periodic addition to the number of individuals who thus fell victims, seemingly, to the "secret curse of the tombs," has served to intensify public interest in this subject until, today, a very large portion of the civilized population of the world believes that the mystery of those deaths has been deliberately protected by science and religion, and by the inconsistent, contradictory, and carefully colored statements of those who know more about it than they care to profess; while a large portion of the uncivilized people significantly shake their heads and intimate that they are entirely too familiar with the subject to risk the displeasure of invisible demons by daring to make any comment.

While feature writers in the Sunday newspapers and in the more or less bombastic magazines have over-exaggerated the historical traditions and well-recorded references to such magical powers, and attempt to frighten the unthinking into strange beliefs, the attempts on the part of prominent scientists and leading spiritual or religious educators to make us believe that the weird, unexpected deaths present merely a chain of coincidences, without any connection with the tomb whatsoever, are just as ineffective in quelling the increasing interest in the possibilities of magical power and its results.

However, some of the foremost mental and psychological experts tell us that if there were any connection whatsoever between the very strange diseases of which each one of the twenty or more explorers passed away suddenly, and the opening of King Tut's tomb and the removal of its mysterious and sacred contents, then that connection was solely mental and consisted of a form of hypnotic suggestion by which each victim created within his body the strange malady from which he died, while still trembling in fear of the thing that he held in his mind as an inevitable punishment for his participation in a violation of an ancient Egyptian law.

Thus an attempt is made to take the mystery out of the category of supposedly ancient magical formulas into the modern category of hypnotic or psychological phenomena, as though this would reduce the whole matter to a readily acceptable and feasible explanation and leave no questions unanswered. If the deaths were due to hypnotic suggestion created in the minds of these explorers as a result of the first and second incidents in the strange chain of mysterious deaths, the cause of the repeated manifestations to the number of twenty-two or more would be wholly within the period of modern times. In other words, if hypnotic suggestion accompanied by fear is the true explanation of the concurring deaths, the cause had its beginning not later than the occurrence of the second, or possibly third, sudden and unexplained death. We might even admit that this psychological cause had its beginning immediately after the first death, but certainly we would not trace this psychological cause to any other incident or fact antedating the strange passing of the first victim of the process.

But the astonishing fact which remains unexplained in such a theory is that the weird circle of mysterious deaths was the precise fulfillment of a prophetic curse uttered and cut into the wall of King Tut's tomb thirty-two centuries ago!

The question then is: what unknown form of magic could carry a curse down through the ages and psychologically produce the physiological results in modern times? Hypnotism or black magic? Necromancy or Karmic law? What have we here that science has not explained, and the lay mind cannot comprehend, but fears?

Another very plausible, though certainly disturbing, explanation has been offered in the suggestion that some chemical poison of a real, tangible material was placed within the sealed tomb of King Tut and deliberately spread upon every article within the tomb and every inch of its walls, and that all of the excavators, explorers, and inspectors who entered the tomb or who handled the funerary articles within it came in physical contact with this poison, which was readily absorbed by their systems, and thus infected them in a manner to produce the almost uniform results in the case of each of the twenty-two victims resulting in the sudden and tragic deaths.

The unthinking mind readily seizes upon this latter explanation as being not only logical but so simple and free from the elements of the supernatural as to be unquestionably correct. But the analytical mind will quickly discover the faults in such a theory. In the first place, experts who have been consulted and who have made the most minute chemical examination analysis of even the dust on the surface of the smallest and largest devices still remaining in the tomb and on the walls of the tomb, and even on parts of the sarcophagus, have failed to find the slightest trace of any poison. And in answer to the question whether some unknown ancient poison might not be hidden in the minute substances tested under the microscope, the experts in the nature of poisons and the pathology of poison claim that there is no poison known to them that would retain its virtue and potency through so many centuries, or which could be so easily absorbed into the system through just the casual contact, with the things in the tomb, made by those who did little more than measure or photograph some of the objects and yet fell victims to the strange disease.

One other outstanding fault, however, makes the foregoing theory of chemical poisoning unacceptable. It is the fact that although all of these excavators and explorers, research men, photographers, artists, and associate observers and witnesses entered the tomb of King Tut at practically the same hour of the same day, and came in contact with the articles within the tomb on the same day, and completed their activities in the tomb on the same day, not all twenty-two were stricken with the disease on the same day nor passed through transition on approximately the same day. Only one by one, with many days, weeks, and months intervening, submitted to the strange malady that brought about the unique deaths. Each one did not manifest the same symptoms except in general classification; each one did not have identically the same pathological or physiological conditions, and each one did not suffer in the same manner. But each one did have precisely the same mental attitude and uncontrollable fear and premonition from the first moment of disability!

And, accompanying the hysterical and uncontrollable fears and as the companion to the horrible premonitions, there were similar visions, hallucinations, and highly illusory psychic states.

What manner of organic or inorganic poison could be manufactured thirty-two centuries ago and so placed in a tomb that it would insidiously affect and inoculate healthy, normal human beings in a few seconds on the same day, and produce in various types of individuals similar physical conditions and precisely the same mental conditions, accompanied by an unusual class of psychic impressions and premonitions, ultimately resulting in incurable physical abnormalities producing horrible deaths, and only one at a time with an indefinite number of days between each?

It is because this last complex question is unanswerable by modern science that the idea or theory of physical chemical poisoning must be abandoned.

If, then, we turn to psychiatrists and the experts in psychological and metaphysical problems and submit the same question, we receive this astonishing answer:

"There is but one insidious poison that could have been invented thirty-two hundred years ago or more, and counted upon to carry out the direful results we have seen, and that poison is mental poison!"

Throughout the ages mental poisoning of one form or another has enslaved millions of human beings and tortured the souls of men and women in all climes and conditions.

Mental poisoning has been the weapon of the earliest and most primitive human creatures. It has been the insidious, invisible, undetectable instrument of torture and death in the hands of the unlearned and the learned, the rich and the poor, the high and the low, and even of those who pose as saintly beings and holy men. It has been the "means to an end" in the hands of evil-minded potentates and rulers, physicians and magicians, priests and clerics, schemers, racketeers, blackmailers and pretending friends.

It has been the scepter of power in the hands of self-appointed leaders of social reforms and organized plunderers.

It is still the subtle, devilish device of millions of men and women who may or may not be wholly aware of its power and its death-dealing potency.

And—all of us from day to day and hour to hour in every walk of life, in every circumstance, are possible victims of mental poisoning unless we understand its nature and can quickly recognize its infectious inoculation and use the only known antidote that will effectively react upon it and leave us uncontaminated!

▽ ▽ ▽

IS BLACK MAGIC POSSIBLE?

———

HROUGHOUT the ages there has been a superstitious belief in the power of the evil eye, the black magician's subtle power, and the hypnotist's dominating mind.

As one journeys through such lands as Egypt in these very modern days, one is impressed with two strange facts. Nearly all of the old native homes or living structures, regardless of their primitive or dilapidated form, have one blue shutter on some window, or, in the absence of any shutters, one blue patch of paint on an outside wall, and there hangs on a cord from the neck of every living creature, including donkeys and camels, and from the neck of most natives, a blue bead. And always the blue is of the same shade—turquoise. The other fact is that most of the men and women in these lands have one of their eyes either totally blind, scarred and injured, or horribly distorted, and this is the case even of little boys and girls. At first one may not realize that there is any relationship between the blue shutter, the blue patch of paint on the wall, the blue bead on the string, and the injured eye. But investigation reveals that all of these things are believed to be absolute protections against the influence of "the evil eye," or the magical influence of some invisible but omnipresent, omnipotent, evil mind.

For centuries the believers in such a superstition took their little infants a few hours or days old and had one eye gouged or burned out with a blunt instrument or even with the fingernail of the *left* hand so that throughout the lives of these children, even unto old age, their horrible appearance would frighten away the evil power, as would the blue shutter, the blue paint, and the blue bead. When we can find such a belief as this still active in uncivilized and semi-civilized lands of today, whose people come in contact yearly with millions of tourists from civilized lands who do not resort to such forms of magical protection, we can understand how difficult it is to remove from the minds and consciousness of human beings any belief that was born in ignorance, fostered by traditions, and seemingly proven by strange coincidences.

In other lands, various forms of incantations, the burning of brush, the sacrificing of little animals, the bathing in strange waters, the torturing of the parts of the body, the wearing or carrying of some amulets or talismans or the drinking of peculiar potions are regarded as sure protections against magical powers of all kinds.

And even in our most modern of civilized countries, among our most intelligent of evolved human beings, we have superstitious beliefs that are just as extraordinary, just as fantastic, and just as inexcusable and unsound as those I have mentioned. Among these strange and superstitious beliefs of the highly educated and evolved nations is that which attributes to certain human individuals the power and the ability to use some magic formula whereby the evil thoughts, the destructive ideas and desires, held within the mind for a brief moment or two, can be radiated or transmitted invisibly and intangibly to the mind and body of another individual at any distance or in any place or circumstance, and take root, become infectious, and proceed to carry out the destructive portent and process of their conception.

According to this still very prevalent superstitious belief, the evil-minded individual of any type or calibre, of any social position, high or low, of any degree of mental and physical prowess, when possessing a wicked heart and some secret formula can deliberately, maliciously, and knowingly, send forth from his mind to the mind, brain, or heart of another being, a stream or ray of thought power that will proceed to destroy the cells of the blood, the cells of the tissue, the cells of the bones, and produce diseases or instant death, or cause the victim to suffer from obsessional ideas that turn into hallucinations, break down and destroy the integrity of the brain, and leave the individual a victim of incurable insanity.

It is almost unbelievable, but nevertheless a fact, that within the cycle of the twentieth century, as in that of the nineteenth and earlier centuries, more new and horrifying books and pamphlets, treatises and lectures, have been written and published, dealing with the practice of black magic, than in all of the centuries of the dark ages.

It is also unbelievable that in recent years certain occult and supposedly white-brotherhood organizations have written and produced in radio stations for nationwide hearing in America, plays and dramas based upon the practice of this black magic, and giving to them all of the atmosphere, all of the dignity, and all of the seeming integrity of truthfulness and logical possibility.

But to the mystic and to the student of Cosmic law and order the belief in such a process of destructive power controlled by any individual is inconsistent, impossible, and truly sacrilegious, and the true mystic and student of Cosmic law is alone capable of rendering judgment in such a case in such a manner. His knowledge and his experience with the divine Cosmic principles enables him to realize and to thoroughly understand that no such process of transmission of destructive energy or power in any thought form between one individual and another or between one individual and a group of individuals would be possible without the conscious approval, aid, and dependable assistance of the universal consciousness and divine spirit that pervades all space and acts as a medium for the transmission of thought waves, light waves, energy waves, or waves of any kind. The belief, therefore, that this divine, Cosmic, Godly-created universal consciousness, put into the universe by the Creator of all that is good, loving, and constructive, for the purpose of unifying all of His harmonious, constructive principles, would lend itself to a process of destruction wholly abhorrent to the universal constructive and creative forces of the universe, and wholly inharmonious to the loving, merciful nature of that consciousness, is a sacrilege as well as an inane and absurd superstition.

In the world of invisible and ethereal radiations of mental concepts, only that which is constructive and truly compatible and harmonious with the nature of God and His consciousness can be transmitted through space from one human consciousness to another, or from the divine consciousness to the human consciousness, or from the consciousness of one living cell to another living cell. Any destructive, incompatible, and inharmonious thought radiation attempting to leave the mind and consciousness of one individual to reach another meets with instant repulsion and immediate dissolution. Its potency is neutralized by the constructive forces and powers of the divine consciousness, and the evil thoughts are forced back into the consciousness of the transmitting mind where the reaction is upon the evil-minded individual, and not upon the intended victim. The mystic and student of divine and Cosmic laws knows that God, in the very beginning of His scheme of creation, made provision that man should be free from mental dominance and control by any mind other than his own. God's whole universe is built upon the principle of creative forces having sole potency in the vibrations of consciousness. The very consciousness of man's mind and body, in every organ and cell, is a part of the consciousness of God, the Father of all living things.

Not a single fact of the belief in the processes of black magic has ever been proved or demonstrated. Why, then, should any human beings or group of them desire to postulate and promote a belief in black magic, or tempt human beings to have faith in such a diabolical agency? The answer is found in the fact that by the promotion and spread of such an idea, accompanied with invented and imaginary demonstrations of it, unthinking persons will voluntarily develop in their own minds and in their worldly objective consciousness a horrible fear of an unknown power, and thus become victims of the fear and of their own self-created destructive thought forms.

He who fears black magic through a sincere belief in its existence and potency, automatically, through self-suggestion within his own mind, becomes not only enslaved by the fear but a ready victim of the evils his mind invents. While the consciousness and Cosmic ether that intervenes between all human beings and fills all space between the souls and bodies of God's creatures on earth will refuse to carry and convey the destructive thoughts held in the mind of one who would use them to injure another, within our own bodies, our own worldly mortal nerves and sensory constitution and physical consciousness will carry from our own minds throughout our own bodies those destructive, inharmonious, infectious and poisonous thoughts that our own minds created out of fear and superstitious beliefs.

Thus we, as individuals, can become the victims of our own poisonous thoughts, but we cannot become the victims of the poisonous thoughts of another. What we may conceive in our minds in fear and through false belief, and allow to become a law and a command unto ourselves, constitutes one form of mental poisoning. All of us are more or less victims of this self-poisoning from the beginning of earthly life to its end, unless we have learned how to protect ourselves against the whole satanic scheme of evil thinking.

But this form of mental poisoning is not the one that is causing and creating, producing and manifesting, throughout modern civilization, the horrible, unfortunate, and unnecessary suffering that makes millions of human beings victims of it hour by hour and day by day. It is with this second form of mental poisoning that we shall deal in the following chapters.

SECTION III

THE PSYCHOLOGY OF MENTAL
REACTIONS

OT many years ago specialists of various kinds were seriously engaged in studying and analyzing reactions to certain nerve stimuli and mental stimuli. In the field of psychiatry and in the field of neurology the common, uncommon, normal and abnormal reactions to the stimuli of various classifications, both physical and mental, or nervous, enabled specialists to diagnose and properly index the physical and mental status of persons who were suffering either from chronic conditions of an unknown origin or strange complexes resulting from suspected causes.

As a result of the many years of analytical study tabulated in minute reports which were gradually brought together and put into a cumulative index of discovered facts, there appeared to be certain forms of reactions which, by their continued manifestation in more than the average case, warranted specialists in calling these reactions the standard or the normal or natural, while all other reactions were looked upon as abnormal, subnormal, extraordinary, or unique.

The actions and reactions of minute animals and household pets were finally involved in the program of scrutiny by the specialists, and we were made acquainted with the psychological as well as the physiological reasons for the little dog striking out in proper method to swim in the lake upon the occasion of his first contact with water. The mystery of his ability to know what to do without any previous instruction and without ever having been in the water before was explained on the basis of reaction to uncommon or abnormal stimuli applied to his nervous system by the sudden contact with the wet and cold water. We learned that the same reactions to unusual stimuli caused the little bird to spread out its wings and attempt to fly when it was pushed away from the edge of the nest for the first time. We gradually learned to understand why children called out in fright at seeing some horrifying picture, or why they so naturally ran to one parent or the other in a moment of seeming danger.

A careful reading of the books dealing with this matter would lead one to think that all of us as human beings, and with the same kind of consciousness in all of our cells, lived and acted and did our thinking and reasoning wholly in accordance with the automatic reactions aroused in our physical, psychic, nervous, or mental systems. The seeking of food when hungry is but a reaction; the desire for drink when the moisture of the body is causing a stimulus upon the part of the nervous system is really another reaction. The pleasure we derive from music or from a ride in the open country or from the taste of some wholesome food or from the smell of a pleasant odor are other forms of reactions resulting from certain specific stimuli.

All of this brought to our understanding some certain fundamental actions on our part that were previously looked upon as primitive, natural instincts. But psychology made plain to us that some of these, such as the automatic attempt to preserve our own selves and our own well-being, were not purely subconscious instincts held over in our present consciousness from the days of our primitive existence. The claim was made by the new school of reactionists that whatever endangered us momentarily acted as a stimulus upon the mental or nervous system and this in turn produced the automatic reaction that manifested itself as an attempt to protect or preserve ourselves.

We have always believed that self-preservation was the first law of conscious existence, and that every living conscious creature from the lowest cell to the most complex group of cells known as the human body would express this instinct when in the face of danger, and do it without having had any special stimulus to bring it about.

But we learn from the psychology of mental reactions, apart from the study of physiological reactions, that there are certain other natural or normal instincts common to all human beings, that may or may not derive from ancient primitive periods of living, but may be a new product of our present higher form of evolved existence. In other words, some such universal instinct among civilized beings may be the direct result of higher evolution of the human consciousness. It may be something born of our modern progress and unfoldment and not of our primitive life.

One such almost universal instinct is to refuse to accept and obey the command of another person without careful analysis and ultimate agreement with the intent and purpose of the command. We do not have to delve deeply into clinical psychology nor spend months and years analyzing the conduct of children in the kindergarten and throughout the years of public school attendance to note that the human mind is reluctant to accept a command from another mind. The natural normal reaction to any external command is most often manifested by the immediate exclamation of the question, "Why?" If two men are walking along the street in opposite directions, and as one approaches the other the one says to the other, "Get off this sidewalk, and let me pass!" the other will react normally and naturally by drawing up his body to its full height and with a glaring look of the eye, manifest this normal instinct of refusal to obey by asking, "Why should I?"

I have used a very unusual illustration to make plain my point, and it is more than likely that if the above incident were to occur in certain places and among certain types of men there would be more reaction than the mere demand for an explanation. Nevertheless, while this illustration is very bold and uncouth, and lacking entirely in subtlety, it does illustrate the principle involved.

Psychology teaches us that the only successful way by which to make another mind or a strange mind obey a wish of our own mind is to present that command or desire in such a subtle manner that it will be either unconsciously or willingly accepted by the other mind and acted upon with cooperation and approval before it has had time to analyze it and resent it. But the instinct to resent a direct command is always present, and this natural and normal resentment must be overcome if we would have other persons do our bidding. That is why, probably, we have gradually developed certain polite formalities in expressing our desires, but even so, a direct command worded in the very finest of polite language would not wholly overcome the natural resentment manifesting itself in a hesitation to obey. If the one man had said to the other, "Will you kindly, my dear and respected sir, venture to step entirely from the sidewalk and allow me ample space to progress on my way!" it is doubtful if the other man would hurry himself out of his position with any more agreeableness than he would have done if requested by the former command. There would be a difference in his reactions undoubtedly, or he would pause a moment to analyze the unusual formula and verbosity of the request, polished with an extraordinary degree of politeness, and come to the conclusion that the individual making the request was either mentally unbalanced or suffering from a superiority complex. In either case, his pause for reflexion and analysis of the request would terminate with the same ultimate reaction of resentment and refusal to move without a further explanation.

But the fact remains as a psychological law that as soon as the average human being is old enough to feel that he is a living entity with certain rights and privileges of his own, he resents almost automatically and most stubbornly any command from an external source that appears to abrogate or take from him or modify his established rights and privileges. Even when these rights and privileges are mistaken ideas and are merely assumed and based upon nothing but personal belief, or even when these rights and privileges are not his at all but are fictitiously assumed for the moment and they are known to be false and unwarranted, still the one who is commanded will resent the right and privilege of the other to make such commands.

A man may step from the graveled paths of a well-kept city park and trample upon the well-cared-for grass lawn with a sign before him to remind him to "Keep off the Grass," and if a civilian like himself approaches him and commands him to "Get off the grass" he will resent the command from the stranger, even though he knows that the command is not an attempt to make him abrogate any of his proper rights, for he knows that he has no right to trample upon the grass lawn. On the other hand, if a police officer or one who is dressed like a park official or caretaker, or someone in higher authority in the city government, for instance, approaches him and gives the same command, he may obey, and obey instantly, but not without the natural resentment that rises up within his consciousness. Recognizing a superior authority does not take from the command the sting it has nor soften the resentment that rises in the consciousness. It simply urges immediate compliance because of that other natural instinct, the *preservation of self*.

We can understand, therefore, why little children when told not to do, or to do, certain things, quickly react and reply with the age-old question, "Why?" The child may not be conscious of the fact that one of his fundamental principles of free action is being jeopardized by the command he receives, but he does sense that the command is a challenge to the conclusion he has reached or the desire he wants to express, or the instinct that he senses, and wishes to carry out to the fullest expression.

Psychologists who have focused their knowledge of mental laws upon the problems of business, such as the problem of advertising and the problem of selling, have taught the astute businessman the ultimate and final psychological lessons that he requires. The businessman—the advertising man and the salesman—has learned that you cannot command potential purchasers to buy things without first anticipating the inevitable question, "Why?" Regardless of the merits of the Steinway or Chickering piano, you could not expect a salesman or advertising man to succeed in building up the merits of such an instrument by publishing in newspapers or magazines or in circulars the forcible command to buy a Steinway piano. If the question of *why* has previously been answered by public statements describing the superior quality of the instrument, the advertising man and the salesman may attempt to rely upon that established knowledge and feel that they can ignore any further explanations of why the piano should be purchased. But it is poor psychology to trust in any person's correct understanding of the merits of any proposition to such an extent as to hope that he will obey a command without further investigation.

A well-known product sold throughout the United States for years was advertised on billboards and in newspapers and magazines solely and exclusively by the statement that, "Eventually (you will buy it) why not now?" This new form of advertising was expected to increase the sale of the good product greatly. But where the advertising appeared in new sections not previously made acquainted with the product, the expected sales did not materialize because it was found that thousands of possible users of the product naturally and unconsciously reacted to the command by asking, subconsciously of course, "Well, why?" What was there about the product that would make an individual inevitably buy it, and why should that individual buy it now? With these two questions left unanswered, the human mind felt the resentment of the command and almost challengingly decided that it would not buy the product. This mental decision, born out of a natural resentment of the command, became a more powerful psychological factor than the original sales command, and was very difficult to overcome except after many years of different advertising.

And so the human race, especially in civilized countries, has proven to be easily affected by its normal and natural instincts and by the psychological processes of its mental reactions. The most successful businessmen, advertising men, psychologists, physicians, surgeons, instructors, teachers, attorneys and professional men in many fields have found that the easiest way, the most efficient way, and the most dependable way to bring about a desired reaction or to have another individual or group of individuals follow a course of action previously outlined for them is to *suggest* it instead of *command* it. And there has risen in the professional fields, especially in the sales and advertising fields, which include part of nearly every art and profession of today, a new school of psychology devoted to the careful study of human reactions and the subtle preparation of forceful suggestions that carry with them all of the potency of a royal command, but all of the agreeableness of a kindly suggestion.

And this school of unique forms of applied psychology has discovered some very fundamental principles. It has found that there are several ways in which very potent commands or suggestions can be given or conveyed by one mind to another, and that there are several ways in which such potent suggestions or actual commands can be and are readily accepted by another mind and almost unconsciously acted upon.

In the long reports of the experts of this new school of applied psychology we come to realize that our daily lives, our daily affairs, our personal, private, intimate and public actions and reactions are almost hourly, and certainly daily, affected by the unsuspected commands and subtly potent suggestions of a horde of highly trained specialists who are working in every field of human interest solely for the purpose of making the rest of us do what they want us to do. They show us that what we eat for our breakfast has been carefully suggested to us but nevertheless commanded. They show us that the articles of clothing we wear and particularly the novel devices from garters to hatpins or types of shoes to cuff links are purchased and used by us, not from any desire born within our own consciousness, but as a result of and reaction to a command subtly created in our minds and acted upon voluntarily. They show that the kind of homes we build, the professions we select for our children, the theaters we attend, the books we buy

to read, the kind of medicine we take, the terminology for the identification of our physical com-
plaints, and even the kind of operations that we
demand in hospitals and the final form and type of
funeral service are the result of desires magically
created in our minds without our least suspicion.
Reading these reports, one begins to wonder whether
any one of us ever has an original idea of his own,
or a desire uniquely conceived and born in his
consciousness without the fatherhood of some mental trickster.

But the analysis of their classifications of methods of producing subtle and effective commands
shows us that there are three methods whereby
the commands or ideas can be conveyed from one
mind to another and accepted by the other mind
almost unconsciously and turned into a law or a
power that instantly sets into motion reactions that
are uncontrollable. The first of these methods of
conveying such potent ideas is by cleverly worded
phrases uttered in unsuspected garb, and offered
with the most agreeable candy coating. The second method is by offering the same idea or the
same thought, with all of its potency, in the form

of an unspoken suggestion, usually by gesture or silence when spoken words were anticipated. The third method is a combination of the first two, but presented in pictorial form either through a drawing, a painting, a motion-picture, or photograph, a diagram, or a list of statistical figures or other symbols.

In fact, the psychology of the process seems to be this: If you can offer a potent idea to another without letting the other person suspect for a fraction of a moment that you are anxious to have him adopt the idea, it will be more readily adopted and accepted and acted upon than if a suspicion is aroused that you are trying to transplant an idea of your own into the other's consciousness. Another very subtle point in connection with this psychological process is that if you, in presenting your carefully veiled command and carefully worded or formed suggestion, can involve it, decorate it, and clothe it so that the other person's mind will hear it or recognize it or see it without immediately understanding its real nature, but will later on evolve it and mature it into a living, vital idea of the individual's mind, then that individual will think or believe that the idea is one of his own conception, his own logical and reasoning conclusion, and (vanity of all vanities) because it is his own conceived and developed idea it must be true and correct and therefore worthy of immediate acceptance and highly enthusiastic adoption.

Reducing all of the foregoing wanderings through the highways and byways of modern psychology—perhaps no more modern than the psychology used by Eve in her explanation of how she came to be serving apples at an afternoon tea in the Garden of Eden—we find that the principle is simply this:

If the individual, Mr. A, wishes to have another individual, Mr. B or Mrs. B, do certain things, believe and feel certain things, and act according to certain fixed ideas, he—instead of going to Mr. or Mrs. B and commanding him or her to do these things, or even politely suggesting them—presents the idea in a roundabout way, perhaps in an allegory, parable, analogy, a citation from something he has read or heard somewhere, or by indirectly referring to a news item in the paper or a wonderful scene in some motion-picture drama now current. He then drops the matter without any indication that he was more than casually interested in it. If, however, he has used the proper psychology in presenting the idea to Mr. or Mrs. B, we will find that a little later on when the two persons are separated and no longer in contact with each other, Mr. B will begin to recall some of the incomplete thoughts given to him by Mr. A and will analyze them, probably trying to solve the mystery of the missing link in the story or trying to find an application of the analogy to present circumstances, and will gradually develop the idea in his own consciousness to a far greater extent than Mr. A presented it to him. Finally—after an hour's time, a day's time or perhaps the passing of a week or a month—Mr. B will discover, as now being interesting to him, some point or some part of the idea that had been presented to him and which he evolved in his own mind to a greater extent, or that may have suddenly quickened into interest by some new incident that had just occurred in his own affairs or his own life or his own body, and instantly he becomes fascinated by the idea and analogy and relationship that he has created in connection with this idea and he reaches a conclusion about it, a decision, and finds in it some essence of a truth. This pleases him and causes him to give more thought to the matter and finally to decide that he has made a discovery or he has evolved an idea that must be of value to him and certainly of significance to him or his mind would not be so occupied with it.

Here is the point where the potency of Mr. A's process reaches its grand climax, for now the command and idea is no longer that which came from Mr. A. The command is no longer something created in the mind of A and passed on to B. It is now the magnificent command of Mr. B's own mind, and of course there can be no rejection and no resentment when the idea is one's own and so gloriously evolved through one's own clever analysis and rational reasoning. So at once the command of A becomes the command of B, and B is within its grasp, within its influence, and unconsciously its victim whether it be for good or evil. This, then, is a part of the psychological process of mental reactions.

STRANGE PROCESSES OF THE
HUMAN MIND

T IS no longer necessary to argue with any sane and thinking person the question as to whether the mind in the human body has any control over the matter that composes the body or the various physiological processes going on within the body. Nor need anyone be a follower of or a devotee to the metaphysical, mystical, spiritual or religious teachings of any sect or cult to recall incidents which constitute proof of the fact that the mind in the human body can be the creator of many strange and peculiar mental conditions.

In the clinical study of the psychological processes formerly called *hypnosis,* it was proved long ago that a person put into an induced state of sleep either by a psychological hypnotic or a chemical hypnotic, and having faith in the integrity and wisdom of the one who induces the sleep, can be made to believe that a cold fountain pen or lead pencil is a red-hot iron. With this cold instrument held before him, and with his believing eyes seeing in it an instrument of torture, it is easy for him to believe also that if this glowing hot piece of metal is touched against his arm for a fraction of a minute, he will suffer intense pain and later have proof of the burn in the form of a water blister on the arm. And in fact, in every test made in this manner during a true state of induced or hypnotic state of belief and susceptibility, the patient in the clinic or science lecture hall has suffered all of the physiological and mental agonies of a burn, even those which would register upon cardiographs or the recording devices of other sensitive electrical instruments.

Sometime after the patient is restored to a normal waking state, although truly unconscious of what has taken place, a water blister of the size and form of the supposed hot metal that touched his arm will form in a very normal and natural manner upon the arm. This may be opened and the water removed from it in the usual manner without any indication to the observer or to the

patient that the very evident water blister was not
the result of an actual physical burn made by contact with an actual hot piece of metal.

We have in this laboratory demonstration that
has been made thousands of times in psychological
clinics in hospitals in Europe and America, and
witnessed hundreds of times by the writer of this
book, an excellent example of how a mental idea,
having no actual or physical basis for its effects,
can create within the human body a truly physiological result. In other words, this demonstration
proves that an idea or a thought in the mind can
translate itself and transform itself into something
that is not merely mental but something as actual
as any actuality that ever affected the human body.

Hundreds of other similar experiments tested on
children, and on adults of all ages and of both
sexes, prove that if the human mind accepts an
idea without question, without doubt, or without
suspicion of any kind, it becomes not merely an
accepted idea but a law, or a command, or a principle that will logically fulfill its purpose and its
nature without any further support in actuality or
in psychological processes.

To make this more understandable, let us recall
the fact that when an actual hot iron or piece of
metal is placed against the arm and we look at it
touching our flesh, we do not have to create in our
minds the idea that it will burn us and will send
torturous impulses of pain up the arm to the brain,
and that we will sense the terrific pain to such an
extent that we will not only feel it but see it re-
acting in contractions of the muscles of the arm
and an attempt of the arm to draw itself away
from the iron. We do not have to create the idea
of withdrawing the arm from the hot iron, for that
idea as a command to the arm is born in the mind
as a result of the pain and suffering that automatically follow the burning of the flesh. And when
the iron has been removed from the arm—or rather,
when the arm has been removed from the presence
of the iron—we do not have to give a mental command to the flesh to form a blister, the shape of the
burn, nor do we have to think of the process that
will follow the burning, such as the forming of a
blister, and so forth. All of these things—the burning of the flesh, the terrific pain, the contractions
of the skin and muscles, the jerking of the arm,

the forming of the blister—follow automatically in due course as logical steps in the process *after* we see the hot iron or feel the hot iron touching the flesh.

It cannot be said, therefore, that the keen twinges of pain, the twitches of the flesh, the contractions of the muscles, the jerking of the arm and the forming of the blister are individual and separate ideas created in the mind and forced into manifestation in the body. Each of the separate steps in the whole process follows successively, automatically as a matter of course, in accordance with nature's laws. The fact that if one hundred arms of one hundred various types of individuals are burned with the same hot piece of metal in the same manner and for the same length of time, we will find similar scars on the tissue caused by the heat and similar water blisters on each of the individuals, shows that nature works very uniformly in these natural processes.

The only difference, therefore, between the whole process of burning the arm with the fountain pen and having it result in a water blister, and burning the arm with an actual piece of hot metal and having it result in a similar water blister, lies in the difference between the concept in the mind in each case. In the one case, the mind of the individual accepted the existence and truthfulness and actuality of the burning metal touching the flesh solely upon the basis of its faith in the integrity of the creator of the idea, and thereafter left nature to carry out its processes in due manner; whereas in the other case the mind accepted the actuality, the truthfulness, the physical existence of the hot iron against the flesh, not upon faith in the integrity of another's mind or another's statement, but upon its own past observation of the iron in its red-hot form, and therefore, the idea of burning being accepted as true, nature's processes were automatically carried out.

We see, therefore, that in both cases the actuality in the existence of the red-hot iron was accepted upon observation. It is generally conceded that "Seeing is believing!"; that if we see a thing we have the very best evidence of its nature, quality and potency to do certain things. In the one case, the patient in the laboratory sees the hot iron through the psychic or psychological eyes of his mind, which are within the mental control of the hypnotic operator. In other words, what the hypnotic operator sees in his own mind and wants the patient to see in his mind is seen by the patient without question or doubt or the least suspicion of deception. Therefore, as far as the psychological processes are concerned, the patient in the induced sleep or hypnotic state does "see" the red-hot iron when the operator tells him that he is holding before him a red-hot iron.

(Right here it may be of interest to students of psychology, and perhaps helpful to those who challenge any of the statements made herein, to know that various tests have proved that while a patient is in an induced sleep, or hypnotic state, his eyes are not blinded as in normal sleep, but are open to physiological perception and to the transmission of light waves or sight waves as in a normal state. However, the interpretation of these impressions is affected by the acceptance of the statements of the hypnotic operator. In other words, when the operator holds before the person who is in the hypnotic state an ordinary bakelite fountain pen or one made of black rubber or one made

of silver metal, and tells him it is a red-hot piece
of iron and suggests to him that he notice its glowing redness, that he notice the little smoke and heat
radiating from it, he can feel the glow of heat
against his face as he stares at it. The hypnotic
subject does see psychologically a change in the
black rubber or silver metal which he saw a few
moments before, or in whatever impression the fountain pen made upon his mind.

There is no change made in the impression
made upon the retina of the subject's eyeball.
Physiologically and in accordance with all of the
laws of physics, a perfect image of the innocent,
cold fountain pen is truthfully cast upon the retina
of the eye. But in our normal waking state as
well as in any hypnotic or psychic state, the process of "seeing" does not end at the retina of the
eye but really is only beginning there, for nerve
stimulations created by the image on the retina
have to be transferred to the psychic or psychological and mental area of the brain and consciousness
where "seeing" becomes more than mere nerve
impulses. Any injury or abnormal physical condition that would disturb the normal psychological

functioning of this area of the brain and consciousness can cause and often does cause erroneous interpretations and translations of the impression
created on the retina of the eye. A person who
is not in a hypnotic sleep or not in a state of sug-
gestibility, or not in the hands of any psychologist,
could look at a piece of black rubber the shape
and size of a fountain pen and "see" a black piece
of metal becoming red hot or glowing with red
heat.

If some cause other than the suggestions of the
operator had led the individual to anticipate that
he was going to be burned with a red-hot piece
of metal, or that there was such a piece of metal
in the room, or that it might be brought before
him for examination, or if he had read and believed for a long time that on certain occasions
individuals were branded with a hot iron on a
certain day of the week when they were found
to be in certain cities or countries and without
employment or home or money, he could react to
these impressions. If he found himself in a hospital or institution on such a day of the week or
year and in such an economical and social condi-

tion and was taken into a room and from some mysterious box the end of a black fountain pen was brought before him and he was asked what he was looking at, he might truthfully say that he was "seeing" a branding iron. Just as a child of two years of age who had never seen a fountain pen might look upon the fountain pen suddenly held before him and call it a piece of licorice candy, simply because while he was actually seeing the same thing that the adult saw, his mind was unable to properly translate the impression on the retina of his eyes into a truthful interpretation.)

This matter of accepting an idea and having that idea carry out its natural process is one of the strange laws of our human brain and consciousness. Whatever idea may be accepted by our brain and our inner consciousness or psychic consciousness or psychological processes of reasoning becomes a law unto us. But that law does not have to be consciously carried out by us through any further conscious efforts that include thinking, analyzing or reasoning. Our inner consciousness or psychic consciousness may do such reasoning and analyzing, but if so, it does it so rapidly, so instantaneously, that we are unaware of it and it is a part of the processes of the subjective or inner consciousness and not a part of the objective or outer consciousness which we use in other forms of reasoning and analyzing.

It is perfectly obvious that if one of us, in our normal, natural waking state, should be shown an ordinary black fountain pen, or let us say the end of the cap that covers the fountain pen, and we were told that it was a red-hot iron, our objective reasoning faculties of the brain would immediately begin to work and by analogy and comparisons determine whether the fountain pen was a red-hot iron or not. The reasoning that the objective brain and outer consciousness would do in such a case would be dependent upon what education the brain had in the past. Of course, if the brain of the individual had never observed or seen a fountain pen before, and if it had never seen a hot piece of iron or any piece of metal that was red hot, or even a piece of wood that was red hot, the objective brain would have no means whereby it could determine by comparison or analogy whether the black object held in front of it was a piece of red-hot metal or not. If he had no knowledge of what was meant by a red-hot piece of metal, he probably would not be disturbed in the least when told that the object was going to be placed against his skin. And even if he were told that the skin would burn, and he had never had any previous burn of any kind, he would not show any reaction to the suggestion or the idea. There would not be the indications of pain and the twitching of the muscles as in the case with the individual who was in the hypnotic sleep. Certainly he would feel the fountain pen against his flesh and it might be of such a moderate temperature that even that impression would be very mild. And if he were blindfolded he probably would not be able to tell just where the rubber shell of the pen was touching him. If, on the other hand, the device was a piece of hot metal, regardless of whether he had ever been burned before or knew anything of the experience of heat against his flesh, the metal would proceed to burn the flesh and there would be all of the twitchings and anguishes of pain as manifested in the case of the cool fountain pen when touching the arm of the one in the hypnotic sleep.

We see, therefore, that an idea implanted in our mind either through observation or through suggestion in the form of words or gestures or otherwise is interpreted by us in the light of our knowledge and past experiences. This was remarkably illustrated in the case of that famous explorer, Livingstone, who went into Africa and on one occasion highly amused the natives by telling them that their heavy, ponderous elephants were able to walk on the surface of frozen water in North America, or in other northern lands. Since even well-trampled ground sank beneath their tread, they could not conceive of a creature weighing many tons walking upon the surface of water without sinking a quarter of an inch into it. Since Livingstone's constant reference to frozen water meant absolutely nothing to natives who had never seen frozen water or "hard" water as they interpreted his words to mean, they simply could not believe that water ever became hard enough or solid enough to hold such heavy creatures, and therefore they could not accept his statement. The words "frozen" and "ice" meant nothing to those who had never seen or experienced these things.

So we find that one of the other strange laws of our human mind and consciousness is that which relates to our individual interpretation of ideas, including things we see or hear, feel, smell or taste. We know when a thing is hot only by our experience with things that are colder, things that are very cold, and things that are very warm. We know what hard and soft may mean only by having had experience with variations in density of articles and variations in the qualities of hardness and softness. It is not true that two individuals will look at the same object and "see" precisely the same thing. Even if there were no variation in the physical impressions cast upon the retina of the eye through light or sight waves, there would still be a difference in the interpretation of those impressions due to a difference in understanding of them because of a difference in education, training, reasoning, and so forth.

But when an idea is accepted by the inner consciousness or the mind and is translated into an understanding of its own, in accordance with its own education and experiences of life, it then becomes to that individual a living, actual thing, in nature and quality, according to the interpretation that the individual's consciousness has given it. From that moment on this living thing is a reality and an actuality, or an actuality with all of the realism that it is possible for it to have in the mind and consciousness of that individual. And this living thing will then produce in the consciousness of the individual all of the actions and reactions that the individual believes and understands should follow thereafter or therefrom.

All of science's investigations and studies of the mental actions and physiological reactions in the human body have shown that nature's regular processes are carried out logically and to the proper conclusion in every case where the idea has been accepted by the mind regardless of whether there was an actuality or a mere illusion or hallucination back of the idea. In other words, if the mind accepted the idea that the fountain pen was a red-hot iron that would burn, that idea became a law and it became a law not only to the consciousness of the

individual but to all of nature's physiological processes, and so long as a red-hot iron will burn the
tissue of the human body, the process of burning will
be carried out, whether the instrument of cause or
the instrument of the idea in the mind was an
actuality or an illusion.

As just one more illustration of this wonderful
process of the consciousness in the human body
and the power of the mind regulating and controlling the physiological processes of the body, or
the matter of which the body is composed, let me
cite the long list of experiments with water made
in various psychological clinics in America and
abroad. With various types of individuals placed
in the satisfactory middle stage of hypnosis, the
temperature of the mouth of each individual was
taken with a two-minute thermometer and carefully established by verification on the part of a
number of witnesses. Then an empty glass was
held before the patient's eyes and he was told that
it was filled with cold, refreshing water. After a
moment's pause in which to allow this idea to become accepted and fixed in the mind, he was told
to take a drink of the water and refresh himself.

The patient would then lift the glass to his lips, bend the head backwards a little, and proceed to swallow the water. A careful counting would show that a swallow was taken about every two and a half to four seconds, and that all the muscles of the throat would act in the typical manner of swallowing water, and one could also see the enlargement of the throat where the water was passing downward in action as in genuine cases of swallowing real water. (If you are unaware of the uniqueness of such a test, hold an empty glass to your own lips and try to imitate a person swallowing water in the normal way, and you will find that it is very difficult to operate the muscles in such a manner and that there is a long pause between each swallow.)

After the patient had what he considered a sufficient drink he would hand the glass back to the operator and smack his lips and in every other manner express and show his appreciation of the cold drink. To prove that his appreciation and experience were not wholly imaginary, based only on the statement of the operator, the thermometer was immediately placed in the mouth again and another two-minute reading taken, resulting in a showing of a lowering of the temperature of the mouth, sometimes as greatly as twenty to twenty-five degrees, but always more than ten degrees. Tests were made at other times to show and conclusively prove that a person in the normal waking state, holding an empty glass to the lips and trying to drink imaginary water, would not draw into the mouth cooling air currents sufficient to reduce the temperature of the mouth more than possibly two degrees.

Whence came, therefore, the drop in temperature or the cooling effect on the tissues and air in the mouth of those persons who drank water from an empty glass? The only possible answer, and one which is in harmony with all of the experiments that have been made in psychological and psychopathic institutions, including those of the Rosicrucian Order and the Rose-Croix University at San Jose, California, is that when the individual accepted the idea that he held in his hand a glass of cold, refreshing water and proceeded to drink it, the idea of cold water coming out of the glass was not merely an idea but a law to all of the natural processes of nature, and to all of the laws controlling the matter and material of his body. Therefore, the law of the idea in his mind proceeded to work in its logical steps and manner of procedure. The muscles carried the water down the throat with the same periodic rhythmic motion with which they always function when actually drinking real water.

The lowering of the temperature in the mouth was but another logical step in the process and not a secondary thought on the part of the patient or the operator. The degree of temperature, however, was affected by the patient's interpretation of what was meant by "a glass of cold refreshing water." If to him the only refreshing drink in the form of water was one of ice water, with perhaps ice floating around in it, then that would be the kind of water he would drink and that would be its temperature, with a resulting reduction of the temperature in the mouth to a very low degree. If, on the other hand, he was not particularly fond of ice water, but enjoyed a drink of cold water just as it comes from the average faucet, then that would be the standard and quality of the idea of water which he would drink. And that would also be the determining factor of the degree of temperature that would register in his mouth.

Here we are face to face, therefore, with some of the strangest laws of God and the universe, but not laws that keep the planets in their courses or cause the earth to move so rhythmically and steadily on its axis or the comets to fulfill their cycles to the precise hour and minute; nor are these the strange laws that govern and control the Cosmic rays and the persistency of racial characteristics in the complex processes of human biology. They are not laws that relate to the unfathomable mysteries of distant space, but laws that relate to our inner selves, our own bodies, our own lives, our very existence. They are laws with which we have to deal minute after minute, day after day, throughout our lives. They are laws that we ought to be more familiar with than any other laws in the universe.

While scientists and explorers may go searching for facts about human existence on the planet Mars or the Moon, or while other explorers may excavate and delve deeply into the buried tombs of Egypt and the forgotten temples of Mesopotamia, few indeed in comparison are giving thought or time to the exploration of the human consciousness and the divine mind in man. We seek mysteries in remote and distant places, and we love to fathom the strange and veiled things of the past and the possible future, but we overlook entirely a marvelous field of exploration that lies within us, and which we can open easily by sitting down comfortably in our own homes and turning our thoughts inwardly and just analyzing the objects that we bring from within the tomb of the self that constitutes the real being.

Strangest of all laws within the body of man! Whatever idea is accepted by our minds and consciousness without suspicion, without doubt, without challenge or without question becomes a law unto our bodies and proceeds to carry out its nature, its purpose, and its natural processes. Whatever idea is acceptable to us translates itself from a purely mental state into a dynamic physical power and force that carries on, unfolds, develops, and proceeds in accordance with principles beyond our control unless we use the same psychological processes to frustrate its activities that were used to bring the idea into existence.

We see, therefore, that man's life and happiness, his health and enjoyment of the things that God has provided, are dependent upon his acceptance of ideas, his understanding of them, his interpretation, and his unconscious submission to their natural development.

Therein lies the secret of mental poisoning!

▽ ▽ ▽

METHODS OF ADMINISTERING
MENTAL POISONING

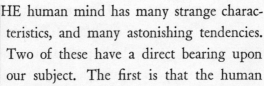

HE human mind has many strange characteristics, and many astonishing tendencies. Two of these have a direct bearing upon our subject. The first is that the human mind or consciousness has a tendency, a very definite impulse, to believe and accept as truth what it wants to believe, or what it feels is a compliment to its ability to reason and reach correct conclusions. The second is an ever-present inclination to accept as a belief, as a truth, as an unquestionable principle, an idea or a conclusion that agrees with another idea or group of ideas previously established in the mind or consciousness from personal experiences.

Either as a part of these two tendencies, or perhaps constituting a third inclination, is that weakness on the part of the human mind and consciousness to prefer to accept and adopt an extraordinary or an uncommon, unique, or distinctly different idea or belief about certain matters, if this unusual idea or belief is compatible with or in harmony with the previous beliefs and ideas held by the mind. In other words, this third tendency, which is really a weakness, is one that seems to give the mind or consciousness of an individual a sort of vainglorious satisfaction in feeling that the individual's previous reasoning and analysis of ideas was better than that of others, or superior to that of others because it has reached a unique conclusion that is different from the opinions held by the mass mind. It is a sort of satisfaction that is born out of such reasoning as: My opinion is right because it is different from the mass, and proves that I am better in my reasoning, keener or more astute in my logical analysis of things, and broader in my mental conception of facts and principles.

Taking this last or third tendency and uniting it with the other two tendencies, we find that the human mind, even in the most uneducated, illiterate, and poorly prepared individual, likes to think of itself as being superior in many respects to the mind of the average person with whom it comes in contact. Such persons love to read the kind of mystery story or detective tale that deliberately reveals between the lines of the first chapter the real personality of the criminal, and yet pretends to include sufficient veiling to make the reader believe, when he astutely discerns the criminal in the first chapter, that the discovery was due to his superior intellect and ability to analyze, and not to any trickery on the part of the writer. But this sort of psychological legerdemain compliments the reader, and when he discovers in the last chapter that his astuteness led him to the right conclusion at the very beginning of the story, he is ready to compliment the writer and acclaim him a clever storyteller and to want to buy and read no other mystery stories except those written by him.

This same weakness tends to make the individual attribute supernatural causes as the explanation of the most common events of life rather than natural causes, solely because the mass mind will look upon the matter differently and cast aside all supernatural considerations. Even when his conclusion of supernatural causes and conditions is scientifically upset, he is ready to denounce the scientists as ignorant, prejudiced, and acclaim himself the better judge. Such persons are otherwise normal in all of their personal daily affairs and in all of their casual thinking and acting, but they love the mysterious because it is so easy to attribute puzzling situations and conditions to unknown, arcane, archaic, or supernatural laws and even to miracles.

In matters of health or business, they are more ready to believe that their trials, troubles, and tribulations are the result of some vague, indefinite, psychic, Cosmic, spiritualistic, or mysterious law or principle at work rather than of any natural law set into motion by their own ignorance or indifference or interference with natural law. They would rather believe that the cold which has been hanging fast and giving them an annoying pain in the chest for so many months is not the result of neglect and indifference on their part, nor due to their having tried to medicate themselves with patented concoctions which they have decided upon after the exercise of their superior reasoning abilities, nor to their having failed to secure proper medical advice and treatment, but to some mysterious moon ray, sunspot beam, planetary conjunction, or psychic visitation.

When they are not believers in these sorts of superstitious principles and powers, they are prone to believe that the "unusualness" of their cold—insofar as it has lingered longer than usually, and has persisted in the face of all forms of self-medication—is due to some strange and weird phenomenon of nature. This may be an unsuspected poison escaping from the illuminating gas used in the home for cooking, or the unsuspected odor or other vibrations from some growing plant that has been within the living rooms for a year or more, or an unnoticed or undetected escape of sewer gas that pervades their home although producing no effect in adjoining homes.

Such persons love to read newspaper advertisements describing patent medicines or commercialized therapeutic specifics that outline the strange symptoms of peculiar maladies. And when they find a suggestion in these advertisements to the effect that some very unusual or uncommon cause, supernatural or mysterious, may underlie their illness, unsuspected by physicians or scientists, they are prone to accept such ideas because they are compatible with ideas previously adopted through their own reasoning.

Whether we like to admit it or not, all of us are prone to think that our own minds, even when we admit that we have not had all of the schooling and education that some have had, are just a little better in certain ways and particularly in discerning the truth behind the veil of mystery. We hesitate to accept the common opinion, the general opinion, the universal conclusion, the most popularly adopted idea, because doing so is not any compliment to our own reasoning and it is never a demonstration of superior thinking. In fact, accepting the general opinion and conclusion regarding any matter always seems to be a frank admission of mental weakness on our part. Therefore, if out of the density and mystery of the complex principles of the universe we can suddenly reach out and pluck a new idea that seems logically to explain the problem at hand, and which grows in its possible correctness the longer we think of it, we like to do so because this is a compliment to our ability to fathom the mysteries of life and to secure and obtain truth through an independent channel. We feel that we are achieving greatness of mind, and incidentally attuning ourselves with the marvels of the unrevealed universe by having stolen from its starry diadem one of its jewels in the form of a unique and original thought.

But these very weaknesses and tendencies on the part of the human mind and consciousness constitute an open portal, an open doorway to the influx and the incoming of strange ideas, and these fertilize the soil of our consciousness and make it highly susceptible to mental poisoning. Unfortunately for the human race, the various kinds of mental poisoning that can ruin and wreck a human life do not have to be administered violently, nor does the individual about to be poisoned have to become hypnotized and placed in an induced sleep nor physically and mentally drugged or overcome in order to have the mental poisoning enter the innermost recesses of the consciousness and begin its destructive work.

It may seem like a paradox and a horrifying incongruity, but it is the truth, that the most violent and virulent of poisons possible to introduce into the human system, into the human mind, consciousness and body, are more easily administered, more readily accepted, more thoroughly absorbed, and more quickly set into disastrous operation than any of the material or chemical poisons known to man, and against which man has spent centuries of time and thought in seeking antidotes and methods of immunity and abortion. He has consistently fought against the germs, microbes, bacilli, and all of the destructive elements that might affect his body slowly or moderately, but he has not spent even a few minutes' thought in making himself immune to the worst of all poisons.

If it were not for the existence of the weakness and tendencies explained above, and for man's readiness to accept mental poisoning, he would not be the victim of the most serious injustices ever committed by man upon man.

Now let us examine some of the types of mental poisons and the manner in which they are administered. First we have the mental poison that produces diseases of the body or certain physical and mental handicaps in the form of chronic conditions. We might call this type of poison Class "A"—not because it is the highest type, the most popular form, or the most universally administered, but simply because it stands foremost in the ease of administration, and is the most horrible in results.

The methods of administering this poison are many, but they fall into three forms: audible suggestions and comments, visual suggestions, and the pictorial and mental. We will proceed with a few typical illustrations.

Number One is a woman nineteen years of age, so normally healthy that any standard insurance company would willingly and readily take a risk on her life by issuing a policy for twenty thousand dollars. She has never been seriously ill, has not inherited anything of a serious nature, is living a normal natural life, and her chances of living to an old age are excellent. She has been riding to work on a trolley car every morning for thirteen months, often catching the same car each morning and becoming familiar by sight with a large number of passengers who have been taking the same car in the same direction day after day. She has noticed for a number of months that a young man who generally sat in the same corner of the car reading the newspaper had found it necessary for some reason to get up from his seat at the end of the first half-hour of the ride and stand on the rear platform, taking deep breaths. At first she wondered whether it was purely physical culture exercise, but her reasoning, always seeking a more mysterious explanation than a common-sense one, told her that he could do the exercises at home and would not have to do them on a streetcar. Her astute reasoning, again seeking for the unusual cause and the unique or original conclusion, decided that perhaps he was afraid of infection and preferred to have better air entering his lungs. This thought brought from the memory storehouse of the young woman, as a recollection, the fact that he had always risen and gone to the rear platform after the car was full of passengers and really overcrowded.

With this suspicion in her mind, she seemed to notice—with that mental ability that wants to build up a mysterious and agreeable conclusion to the previous thoughts—that he was becoming a little paler each day, and seemed to be a little weaker when he rose from his seat and forced his way out to the rear platform. And did he not seem to stagger a little with weakness on several occasions when he stepped from the trolley car platform at the end of the trip? Then one day a woman of about forty years of age seated at the opposite end of the trolley car fainted. Her face appeared to be as pale as that of the young man on the rear platform. She was taken from the car to a nearby drugstore to be revived and cared for, and the trolley and its passengers went on.

The next day she was back in her usual position in the car, but did she not seem to be a little paler than on previous days? Then one morning our young lady noticed that both the young man and the woman of forty were absent. What could have happened? The desire to solve a mystery arose in the young girl's consciousness; the desire to have a real mystery come out of a problem rose to supreme heights. The absence of these two persons *must* be connected with all of the preceding incidents that had been noticed. Illness of some kind had overcome them, and that illness had been something contracted in the car, slowly but surely.

The young woman reached her office and began to reason. Was it true that overcrowded places were incubators of germs and disease? Were the editorial writers and health writers in popular magazines correct in their contentions? Was she herself becoming affected by this very injurious and unhealthful ride every morning? She rushed to a mirror to observe her complexion. Yes, she was paler than she should be! Should she go and see a doctor? What could she tell him? She had no symptoms, no aches or pains, and of course he would not believe the strange and mysterious fact that she had developed in her mind from careful observation. He might even laugh at her idea. She would wait and see if anyone else became ill. Three days later, on leaving the trolley car, she determined to settle the mystery by asking the conductor if he knew why the two persons no longer rode with him on that car. His answer: "The young man died two days ago from a gradual weakening of his heart and lungs. His brother, a policeman who rides sometimes on this car, later in the morning, told me that the young fellow died before they could determine whether it was tuberculosis of an unsuspected nature or heart disease. The only thing they were sure of was that he had picked up some germs during the day while going to or from work or while at work. The woman, I understand, is sick with scarlet fever which she contracted somewhere during the past few weeks. The Board of Health was very much concerned over the fact that she was riding up and down in this car for many days while she was in the early stages of the disease. The car has been disinfected three times."

Horrors! The young woman's worst suspicions were confirmed. Riding in the trolley car was more than dangerous. It was suicide. No wonder she looked so pale. During that morning there were three distinct times when she felt a sort of swimming sensation, a dizziness, a weakness in her head and body. At noontime she spoke to a woman friend about it. Said the woman friend: "Didn't you see in the papers that there was an epidemic of scarlet fever in the Fulton section of the city, and isn't that where your trolley car starts from each morning with some of its passengers in it? Don't you know that more diseases are picked up in subways, elevated trains and trolley cars in New York and other cities than anywhere else? Why, these terrible germs are picked up so gradually that you never notice you are becoming sick until finally you see a little paleness coming in your face, and then some day you begin to feel a dizziness and a weakness of the brain and body. That weakness means that the disease has attacked the brain, and then it is too late for anyone to do anything. Even inoculation cannot save you when the brain becomes affected through your breathing and inhaling the germs in such crowded places with such foul air. I hope that you never contact any of the germs, because you are so young, and young people between seventeen and twenty generally die of scarlet fever. I ought to know, because I lost a sister who was a school teacher, and who developed the germs in just that manner from some of the pupils in her class. They were saved, but my twenty-year-old sister died."

Three days later the young lady began to have daily fainting spells and spells of dizziness. Hoping that she might be saved without the painful process of inoculations and spinal or other injections, she went to a physician, merely telling him of her symptoms and not of her suspicions. Finding no real cause for dizziness, he said: "There seems to be some mysterious or subtle influence affecting your nervous system, and I must wait until something more develops before I can give you a correct diagnosis, but in the meantime I will give you this prescription which will purge your system and cleanse your blood."

As each day passed, the fainting spells became worse, the face paler, the body weaker. In two weeks the young woman was worrying her family by being bedfast, with fever, a wandering mind, delirium, and a rapid pulse. Finally, in one of her spells of delirium, she muttered, "I know it is scarlet fever. I got it in the car, but I must not let anyone know. Don't tell the doctor! Two of them have died; I will be the next." The family told the physician of the strange words they had heard her utter. The next day the girl heard the physician say in a whisper, just outside the door of her room: "If it is scarlet fever, it is of the brain-fever classification, and at her age may be fatal. She must have reached the crisis by this time, and if she has, she may become worse every minute and must be carefully watched tonight!"

Within twenty-four hours the young woman was in such delirium that the family became frantic and sent for a specialist, who recognized in her mutterings the symptoms of something psychological rather than physiological. He saw the symptoms of the form of mental poisoning that obsessed her. It was like a demon within her consciousness bent on destroying her from within. It was like some evil spirit that had come upon her which must be destroyed in the same way as used by Jesus when He enjoined His disciples to cast out evil spirits and demons in order that the sick might become healed and cured.

The specialist secured the cooperation of an eminent psychologist, and with the help of the physician, the three were able to bring the young woman gradually back to health. For months there lingered in the mind and consciousness of

the young woman the horrible picture of germs
floating around in the trolley car entering her
body through the nostrils and the mouth, destroying the blood cells, attacking the brain tissues,
gradually casting her mind into a state of coma
from which she was rescued by what was called
a miracle.

When was the mental poison administered, and
how? The first dose of the poison was administered by the conductor, by his casual, logical story
that seemed to fill in the gaps in the mystery that
she had created in her own mind. Everything the
conductor told her fitted in magnificently with her
own conclusions. Therefore, his story must be the
truth! The second administration was a visual
one of her own appearance, then a sensuous one
of her own weakness and dizziness. But the most
overpowering draft of the mental poison was administered by the woman friend who cleverly
(though certainly not maliciously) described the
manner in which the scarlet fever "germ" can at-
tack the brain, and how it can be picked up in
trolley cars and subways and how it was already
spreading in the city, especially that part from

which the trolley came, and how her sister had died because she was twenty years of age! And then the final dose of the poison was administered by the physician who uncautiously, unthinkingly, made statements in the presence of the keen hearing of the suspicious girl. Few persons realize how keen is the hearing of the sick patient who is fearful that the truth has not been told to him, or that there is some mysterious element about his condition.

The one whose mind is weakened, or the one whose mind is broken down, who appears to be mentally stupid, unsound or insane, is keenly aware of every sound, every motion, every gesture, every suggestion, every thought.

And so the young woman was about to go to her grave, not from imaginary conditions but from actual ones. Her weaknesses, her fevers, her deliriums, were not hallucinations, not mere mental states that psychological suggestions would wipe out in a few hours or that mental affirmations would correct in a few days. They were physiological, pathological conditions that had a real histology back of them, and yet could not be corrected by the ordinary or usual medical system of therapy. There is no known drug or herbal extract or material essence or compound that is a true antidote for mental poison. It can be neutralized and overcome only by an antidote of a sane mental nature, divinely inspired, properly administered by sympathetic and loving minds who understand and are prepared to fight the processes of mental poisoning.

Sometimes the efforts of those who believe that they can overcome this poison with counter-suggestions, with joking and laughing attitudes, with statistics and arguments, simply cause the administration of more poisoning. They lead the patient to think that they suspect the mind of the patient is weak or unsound and that such arguments and methods of counteraction are necessary; or they cause the patient to think that the case is more serious than it appears and is therefore beyond the hope of medicine or surgery and that some unusual or mysterious mental process must be used to fight it. So the most loving and sympathetic and kindly of friends and professional people with the best intentions may become poisonous, and administrators of mental poisoning, without intention.

Another illustration, quite common and universal, is that of an actual physical weakness of more or less common cause, existing in the body of one who does not suspect the real nature but reads advertisements and health articles in an attempt to diagnose the conditions and discover a real cause for the occasional pains or symptoms. The longer the search for a correct diagnosis, and the longer remedies are tried without success, the more sure becomes the opinion that the illness is of a very deep nature and wholly uncommon, and the result of some strange or peculiar combination of conditions.

This conclusion is accepted by the mind and causes reactions, as explained in the preceding section of this book, with the result that actual physiological complications are set up that are difficult to analyze, and more difficult to treat. The patient then begins to seek for an understanding by searching among the accounts and records, the explanations and pictures of rare diseases. Suddenly a series of symptoms are presented in some patent medicine advertisement or some health article that wholly agree with the symptoms which the patient has suspected and immediately there is established a conviction that the disease referred to in the advertisement or news article is identical with the one from which the patient now suffers. The acceptance of such a thought establishes a law of action in the body, and the mind proceeds to build up and create the identical symptoms which have been mentally accepted.

In the still further search for more light and information, the patient rejects every explanation that attributes the pains and conditions to natural causes easily overcome, and looks only for those causes and conditions which are deep-rooted, mysterious, and always serious and vital. Hour after hour the mind of the patient is concentrated wholly upon that area or that part of the body where the disease is suspected of existing. The pains may be general throughout the torso of the body. They may at times seem like cramps. There may be cutting sensations like those produced by gastritis, or so-called gas in the intestines, or by cold and inflammation of the intestines, or by any number of other temporary or common abnormal conditions or causes of abnormal conditions. But the mind is concentrated upon the gall sac with the conviction that there are stones in the sac, and that these are solely responsible in accordance with what the patient has read and then concluded in her mind.

Every ache and pain in any part of the body is immediately traced mentally to the gall sac. Every flush of the temperature of the blood, every little mental excitement that causes a change in the pulse, is immediately attributed to the gall sac and the presence of stones in it. A search is made through medical books in libraries, through all the health magazines sold on the newsstands, through every patent medicine circular or pamphlet that may be secured, for more light on the subject of gallstones. Every unusual word or every word susceptible of having a double meaning is created into a definition or term for gallstones. Every symptom described that the patient does not have is cast aside as inconsequential. Every symptom mentioned that is somewhat like those which the patient has is enlarged and magnified into a symptom of an identical nature. The descriptions of the gallstones in their process of formation are visualized and re-created in the mind and finally by mental reaction actually created in the gall sac.

The gall sac does become affected, not in the manner that the patient believes, not to the extent that the patient has suspected, but through mental poisoning, with all of the symptoms and all of the pathological and physiological conditions and actions and reactions that any patient has ever suffered from gallstones. Day after day the stories of other persons suffering from gallstones, the sudden deaths of persons suffering from unknown conditions, the pains of years ago, the unusual diseases of the grandfather and the grandmother, and hundreds of other things are focused into one point within the patient's body—the gall sac, with the stones in it. And day by day the mental poison is administered by reading, hearing of stories and reports of statistics, and by the illogical reasoning of the patient. The patient becomes a chronic sufferer, and the fact that physicians can do nothing for her, can find no actual gallstones, or can find nothing that will affect the pains in the gall sac or the rest of the body, constitutes more proof that the condition is serious and therefore deeply hidden. A chronic condition is established, and it grows and grows, and as long as the mind of the patient is capable of accepting and receiving more mental poison, the patient will become worse and worse until transition results.

But the worst cases of mental poisoning are those that are either deliberately, maliciously, or unsympathetically administered by friends or acquaintances, who pretend to have knowledge or who pretend to have a keen insight into the mysteries of health and disease, and who are so glib and voluble in their explanations and so ready to tell another person why he has a slight pain or a slight ache, or a slight abnormality.

When we realize that there is no such thing as a perfectly normal body at any age, or that there is no time at any hour of our lives when every part of the body is in a perfectly normal condition, and when there is no congestion, no clogging, no lack of anything, no overabundance of anything, no pressure, no strain, no unnecessary tenseness, no weakness; when we realize that each and every one of us has some part of our body just on the verge of resenting some violation of nature or kicking back at some wrong that has been committed, or protesting against some food that has been eaten or some liquid that has been drunk, and when we realize that there is hardly a week in the year when some part of our body and our system is not fighting some germs that have been taken in through breathing, drinking, or eating, and that this tax upon the blood stream and the heart may cause peculiar sensations that are neither serious nor important, but which can easily be interpreted as something wrong and direful, it is not to be wondered at that the human mind with its constant concern for health, with its fundamental desire to maintain and preserve the body and all of its faculties and powers, is a fertile ground for any idea or thought that may be administered without careful analysis and mental filtration.

It is, therefore, easy to understand how an individual, anxious to know why or how certain light or casual disturbances within his body may have occurred, or what they are leading to, may be wrongly directing his thinking and have his whole process of analysis poisoned by the administration of mental poisoning at the hands of some friend, some relative, some acquaintance, or even some physician or scientist, who speaks unguardedly or unthinkingly, and who may accidentally and innocently administer the most virulent and destructive dosage of mental poison in a casual remark, or in a long speech intended to illuminate the mind of the patient.

Then there are those kindly women who love to tell the expectant mother what dreadful days await her, and of what serious complications are likely to set in overnight, and of what unexpected consequences may follow her perfectly normal and natural condition! They delight in recounting to the new mother, the inexperienced one, the hopeful and optimistic one, how serious a mistake it is to be too optimistic and to count too much on the assurances of the physician or to put any reliance upon the family history and ancestry. They love to dig out of the misty, shadowy alcoves of the past the few extraordinary and most unusual cases that should have long been forgotten, and most of which perhaps never happened, wherein the healthy, normal expectant mother was suddenly visited by horrible complications that brought about blood poisoning or injury to the mother and child resulting either in the birth of an abnormal child or a monstrosity, or the death of both mother and child. They love to emphasize the fact that in the last fifty years there have been several hundred strange deaths at the time of confinement, without even mentioning that in the same period of time there were perhaps millions of births that were perfectly normal, or without mentioning the fact that in the unusual and disastrous cases the mothers were of an abnormal structure or of long-diseased blood condition or of most unusual inherited tendencies.

These administrators of mental poison seem to be jealous of the possibility that the young and innocent, trustful and hopeful expectant mother before them may have that beautiful, normal confinement that the average woman has. They seem

to take a delight in seeing the brow of the expectant mother wrinkle, the eyes sadden, the lips quiver
as they predict the horrible possibilities that may
await her.

And woe be unto the poor young mother if
she admits to one of these mental poisoners that
the day before yesterday she hit her left elbow
against the faucet in the kitchen sink, or that in
going down the steps her left heel caught and
for a moment she stumbled, but never fell or
never struck her body; or that the other night in
the midst of her sleep she awakened by feeling
a peculiar pain for the first time between the
ribs of her left side, or that the little toe of her
left foot had a cramp in it, or that one of her
teeth seemed to ache a little the last few days.
Each and every one of these innocent incidents,
wholly unconnected with the process of gesta-
tion, are instantly magnified and pointed out to
the young hopeful as sure indications of a serious situation, and incidents are related where
persons of their acquaintance who had similar
pains, aches, knocks or bruises had the most horrible results in the confinement room of the hos-

pital. They love to see the young mother walking away burdened as with a heavy cross from the dose of mental poison they have just administered. And if that poor mother does have a little more pain or some little unfortunate incident connected with the birth of her child that neither physicians nor nurses think seriously enough of to tabulate in their reports, one of the administrators of the mental poisoning is sure to seize hold of it and say, "I told her so, and she will have even worse than that with her child!" And the story will go around to other expectant mothers, with the astonishing claim that her previous predictions to other expectant mothers had been verified, and thus the dose of poison to the second one is strengthened by little incidents that occur during the birth of the child in the first case of mental poisoning.

And there are on record plenty of those other cases of mental poisoning where a malicious mind, a demon incarnate if ever there were such a thing, has gone forth to ruin and destroy the life of a friend or foe, of an acquaintance, of one who has crossed his or her path. Both men and women have deliberately concocted dosages of mental poison and have gone out of their way to administer them to the innocent victims. They have not only sown seeds of distrust in the minds of those who have had faith and confidence in employees and friends, but they have deliberately served mental potions of virulent poison in the form of suggestions that had all of the semblance of truthfulness, and which would find some verification in plausibility in the mind of the victim until he or she would say unto himself: "He is right! I have never thought before of that fact and this fact and the other fact as being connected, but now I see how they are, and I see now that I have been and still am a victim of conditions over which I have no control. This will guide me into the gutter, wreck my life, disgrace me and my family, and bring complete ruination. It is too late; I am done for."

In twenty-five years or more, during which men and women of all types, of all walks of life, of all professions and social standing have written me of their problems and have had interviews, seeking as the last straw a way out of their horrible dilemmas, I have found that fully seventy-five per cent of them were suffering more from conditions that did not exist, except in their minds, than from anything else. Even when their situations or conditions were founded upon some actual occurrence that was in itself more or less direful, the way out of the problem, the solution of it, the logical, reasonable correction and alteration of the conditions, was wholly held up, completely inhibited, and fearfully suspected, because of some administration of mental poison on the part of someone who wanted them to be hopeless, despondent, pessimistic and hesitant in attempting to redeem themselves or bring about any change in the unhappy conditions. I have found them held in the grasp of false beliefs administered in a poisoning manner to such a degree that they could not even see their own problems in the proper light, that they no longer had any faith in kith or kin, in friend or even in professional and expert guidance and advice. Yes, some have even doubted the existence of God, or that there was any mercy or justice in the world.

While it is true that many of us with the most

kindly, loving and eleemosynary natures may at times make a remark or offer a suggestion or send forth a thought or an idea or a mental picture that is immediately misunderstood or misinterpreted and turned into a dose of poison that begins at once its process of inhabiting and affecting the mind of our listener, it only illustrates the necessity that exists for our careful consideration of the thoughts we create in our own minds, and which we allow to escape in the presence of others in the form of words or gestures or subtle suggestions of one form or another.

I recall having once been at the bedside of a woman who had been ill long enough to suspect that her heart was weakening, and that the end was close at hand. She insisted that the nurse call for a physician at once to test her heart and her breathing. As I stood by I saw the physician enter the room and take from the pocket of his large white smock a folded stethoscope. I saw him try to adjust it rapidly and put it into working condition and hurriedly apply it over her heart while he tried to listen. But I saw that one of the pieces of rubber tubing was hopelessly twisted, and as he tried to listen he suddenly saw that himself and rapidly jerked the stethoscope from his ears and from the body of the patient. He threw it toward the nurse with a whispered request that she go out of the room and get him another one.

The patient, who had been watching the physician with that extreme anxiety that bordered on the verge of ultimate mental strain, saw him jerk the instrument away and turn toward the nurse with a dissatisfied attitude, and she immediately exclaimed: "O my God, is it too late?" And she immediately went into a mental and physical state that bordered on a coma, and she had so shocked and poisoned herself by accepting a dose of poison that was not intended to be such that it was many weeks before she was restored to a normal condition, and she might very easily have passed through transition at the moment she threw herself into the hysterics.

The kindly physician did not know that his unfortunate action in pulling away the stethoscope and casting it at the nurse behind him was a mental suggestion to the patient that her heart had stopped, that he could not hear the heart, and that there was no use in trying to hear it. Such is the readiness of the human mind not only to accept subtle suggestions, but to misinterpret them, and to adopt them as a law, a command to the physical body to abide by the conclusion of the suggestion.

For these reasons and many more it behooves every man (and woman) carefully to guard his thoughts, his words, his gestures, and his actions. The human mind is more sensitive than either the most sensitive of photographic films or the most sensitive of microphones. Care is taken on every motion picture lot that automobiles on its streets are stopped, that persons who are hammering out of doors or walking on graveled paths or whispering on the set, become silent while out-door scenes are shot, until a whistle is blown or a bell is rung indicating that the microphone is no longer in operation. It will pick up delicate sounds from hundreds of feet away and ruin the scenes under production. The new candid cameras with their ultra-sensitive lens and films will register in one-hundredth of a second the slightest motion, even in shady or dimly lighted places. But the quickness of the lens and the film and the sharpness and keenness of the microphone are as nothing compared to the power of registration possessed by the human mind. It can see in the look and glance of one eye toward another, in the quivering of a lip, in the trembling of a hand, in the tone of a voice, in the choice of words, in the connection of ideas, expressed or gestured, a meaning, an interpretation, a suggestion, that may be like unto the most powerful of destructive winds.

On the other hand, we also possess, through these same mental powers and faculties, the abilities to send forth good, constructive, cleansing, re-creating, regenerating ideas, suggestions, or commands—which are presented in the same sincere and subtle manner so as not to arouse suspicion of their purpose—that will bring health and happiness, hope, ambition, and determination even to the most afflicted and weakened human beings. We can dispense cheer instead of sorrow. We can administer hope instead of despondency. We can pour into the mind and consciousness of another a smiling attitude, an increasing determination of will power, a picture of a bright future, an open doorway to opportunity, a cleansing power that will reach every part of the body and a divine effulgence of spiritual joy that will rejuvenate and redeem the most hopeless of creatures.

And when, over thirty-one centuries ago, the wise psychologists and Magians whose duty it was to protect the tombs of their beloved kings, carved upon King Tut's tomb the warning, the command, the positive statement, that whosoever wilfully violated the sacred laws of Egypt and maliciously forced themselves into the sealed chamber should suffer the curse of the gods and die, they administered then and there a dose of mental poison to unknown future victims, who, by their own wilful acts after having read the warning, deliberately accepted the poison and allowed it to become a law and a command unto them, even unto death.

▽   ▽   ▽

Explanatory

▽

THE ROSICRUCIAN ORDER

ANTICIPATING questions which may be asked by the readers of this book, the publishers wish to announce that there is but one universal Rosicrucian Order existing in the world today, united in its various jurisdictions, and having one Supreme Council in accordance with the original plan of the ancient Rosicrucian manifestoes. The Rosicrucian Order is not a religious or sectarian society.

This international organization retains the ancient traditions, teachings, principles, and practical helpfulness of the Brotherhood as founded centuries ago. It is known as the *Ancient Mystical Order Rosae Crucis,* which name, for popular use, is abbreviated into AMORC. The international jurisdiction of this Order for North, Central, and South America, British Commonwealth and Empire, France, Switzerland, Sweden, and Africa is located at San Jose, California.

Those interested in knowing more of the history and present-day helpful offerings of the Rosicrucians may have a *free* copy of the book entitled, *The Mastery of Life,* by sending a definite request to SCRIBE W. C. A., AMORC Temple, Rosicrucian Park, San Jose, California.

∇ ∇ ∇

The Rosicrucian Library

Consists of a number of unique books which are described in the following pages. If your regular book dealer does not have these books in stock, and you do not care to wait until he secures them for you, you may save time by sending your order direct, with remittance or C.O.D., postage prepaid by us.

ROSICRUCIAN SUPPLY BUREAU
Rosicrucian Park, San Jose, California, U.S.A.
or
25 Garrick Street, London, W.C. 2, England

∇ ∇ ∇

VOLUME I

Rosicrucian Questions and Answers with Complete History of the Order

By H. SPENCER LEWIS, F.R.C., Ph.D.

▽

THIS volume contains the first complete, authentic history of the Rosicrucian Order from ancient times to the present day. The history is divided into two sections, dealing with the traditional facts and the established historical facts, and is replete with interesting stories of romance, mystery, and alluring incidents.

This book is a valuable one since it is a constant reference and guidebook. Questions that arise in your mind regarding many mystical and occult subjects are answered in this volume.

For many centuries the strange, mysterious records of the Rosicrucians were closed against any eyes but those of the high initiates. Even editors of great encyclopedias were unable to secure the fascinating facts of the Rosicrucian activities in all parts of the world. Now the whole story is outlined and it reads like a story from the land of the "Arabian Nights."

The book also outlines answers to scores of questions dealing with the history, work, teachings, benefits, and purposes of the Rosicrucian fraternity. It is printed on fine paper, bound in silk cloth, and stamped in gold. Price, postage prepaid, $2.85 (£ 1/1/- sterling).

VOLUME II

Rosicrucian Principles for the Home and Business

By H. Spencer Lewis, F.R.C., Ph.D.

▽

THIS volume contains such principles of practical Rosicrucian teachings as are applicable to the solution of everyday problems of life, in business and in the affairs of the home. It deals exhaustively with the prevention of ill-health, the curing of many of the common ailments, and the attainment of peace and happiness, as well as the building up of the affairs of life that deal with financial conditions. The book is filled with hundreds of practical points dealing especially with the problems of the average businessman or person in business employ. It points out the wrong and right way for the use of metaphysical and mystical principles in attracting business, increasing one's income, promoting business propositions, starting and bringing into realization new plans and ideals, and the attainment of the highest ambitions in life.

Rosicrucian Principles for the Home and Business is not theoretical but strictly practical, and is in its ninth edition, having had a wide circulation and universal endorsement not only among members of the organization, who have voluntarily stated that they have greatly improved their lives through the application of its suggestions, but among thousands of persons outside of the organization. It has also been endorsed by business organizations and business authorities.

The book is of standard size, well printed, bound in silk cloth, and stamped in gold. Priced, postage prepaid, $2.95 (£1/1/9 sterling).

VOLUME III

The Mystical Life of Jesus

By H. SPENCER LEWIS, F.R.C., Ph.D.

▽

THIS is the book that thousands have been waiting for—the real Jesus revealed at last! It was in preparation for a number of years and required a visit to Palestine and Egypt to secure a verification of the strange facts contained in the ancient Rosicrucian and Essene records.

It is a full account of the birth, youth, early manhood, and later periods of Jesus' life, containing the story of his activities in the times not mentioned in the Gospel accounts. The facts relating to the immaculate conception, the birth, crucifixion, resurrection, and ascension will astound and inspire you. The book contains many mystical symbols, fully explained, original photographs, and an unusual portrait of Jesus.

There are over three hundred pages with seventeen large chapters, beautifully printed, bound in silk, and stamped in gold.

Here is a book that will inspire, instruct, and guide every student of mysticism and religion. It is one of the most talked-about books ever written on the subject. Read it and be prepared for the discussions of it that you will hear among men and women of learning.

Sent by mail, postpaid, for $2.95 (£1/1/9 sterling).

VOLUME IV
The Secret Doctrines of Jesus
By H. SPENCER LEWIS, F.R.C., Ph.D.

▽

DOES the Bible actually contain the unadulterated words of Jesus the Christ? Do you know that from 325 A.D. until 1870 A.D., twenty ecclesiastical or church council meetings were held, in which *man* alone decided upon the context of the Bible? Self-appointed judges in the four Lateran Councils expurgated and changed the sacred writings to please themselves. The Great Master's *personal* doctrines, of the utmost, vital importance to every man and woman, were buried in unexplained passages and parables. *The Secret Doctrines of Jesus,* by Dr. H. Spencer Lewis, eminent author of *The Mystical Life of Jesus,* for the first time *reveals* these *hidden truths.* Startling, fascinating, this book should be in every thinker's hands. It is beautifully bound, illustrated, of large size, and the price, including postage, is only $2.95 (£1/1/9 sterling).

VOLUME V

"Unto Thee I Grant . . ."

By Sri Ramatherio

▽

THIS is one of the rarest Oriental mystery books known. It was translated by special permission of the Grand Lama and Disciples of the Sacred College in the Grand Temple in Tibet.

Here is a book that was written two thousand years ago, but was hidden in manuscript form from the eyes of the world and given only to the initiates of the temples in Tibet to study privately.

Out of the mystery of the past comes this antique book containing the rarest writings and teachings known to man with the exception of the Bible. Hundreds of books have been written about the teachings and practices of the *Masters of the Far East* and the adepts of Tibet, but none of them has ever contained the secret teachings found in this book. The book is divided into many parts, each part containing a large number of sections or divisions and chapters.

The book deals with man's passions, desires, weaknesses, sins, strengths, fortitudes, ambitions, and hopes. All are treated in detail with illuminating simplicity. The book is beautifully printed and bound with stiff cover, and contains also the strange mystic story of the expedition into Tibet to secure this marvelous manuscript.

Price, per copy, postage prepaid, only $1.90 (14/– sterling).

VOLUME VI

A Thousand Years of Yesterdays

By H. Spencer Lewis, F.R.C., Ph.D.

▽

Here is a book that will tell you about the real facts of *reincarnation*. It is a story of the soul, and explains in detail how the soul enters the body and how it leaves it, where it goes, and when it comes back to earth again, and why.

The story is not just a piece of fiction, but a *revelation of the mystic laws* and principles known to the Masters of the Far East and the Orient for many centuries, and never put into book form as a story before this book was printed. That is why the book has been translated into so many languages and endorsed by the mystics and adepts of India, Persia, Egypt, and Tibet.

Fascinating—Alluring—Instructive

Those who have read this book say that they were unable to leave it without finishing it at one sitting. The story reveals the mystic principles taught by the Rosicrucians in regard to reincarnation as well as the spiritual laws of the soul and the incarnations of the soul.

It is well printed, bound with a cloth cover, and worthy of a place in anyone's library.

Price, per copy, postage prepaid, only $1.90 (14/– sterling).

VOLUME VII

Self Mastery and Fate with the Cycles of Life

By H. Spencer Lewis, F.R.C., Ph.D.

THIS book is entirely different from any other book ever issued in America, dealing with the secret periods in the life of each man and woman wherein the Cosmic forces affect our daily affairs.

The book reveals how we may take advantage of certain periods to bring success, happiness, health, and prosperity into our lives, and it likewise points out those periods which are not favorable for many of the things we try to accomplish. It does not deal with astrology or any system of fortunetelling, but presents a system long used by the Master Mystics in Oriental lands and which is strictly scientific and demonstrable. One reading of the book with its charts and tables will enable the reader to see the course of his life at a glance. It helps everyone to eliminate "chance" and "luck," to cast aside "fate," and replace these with self-mastery.

Here is a book you will use weekly to guide your affairs throughout the years. There is no magic in its system, but it opens a vista of the cycles of the life of each being in a remarkable manner.

Well printed, bound in silk cloth, and stamped in gold to match other volumes of the Rosicrucian Library. Price, postage prepaid, $2.85 (available in London, 16/6 sterling).

VOLUME VIII

Rosicrucian Manual

By H. SPENCER LEWIS, F.R.C., Ph.D.

▽

THIS practical book contains not only extracts from the Constitution of the Rosicrucian Order, but a complete outline and explanation of all the customs, habits, and terminology of the Rosicrucians, with diagrams and explanations of the symbols used in the teachings, an outline of the subjects taught, a dictionary of the terms, a complete presentation of the principles of Cosmic Consciousness, and biographical sketches of important individuals connected with the work. There are also special articles on the Great White Lodge and its existence, how to attain psychic illumination, the Rosicrucian Code of Life with thirty laws and regulations, and a number of portraits of prominent mystics including Master K. H., the Illustrious.

The technical matter contained in the text and in the hundred or more diagrams makes this book a real encyclopedia of Rosicrucian explanations, aside from the complete dictionary of Rosicrucian terms it contains.

The *Rosicrucian Manual* is of large size, well printed, beautifully bound in red silk cloth, and stamped in gold. The book has been enlarged and improved in many ways since its first edition.

Price, postage prepaid, $3.10 (£ 1/2/9 sterling).

VOLUME IX

Mystics at Prayer

Compiled by MANY CIHLAR
Austrian Philosopher and Mystic

▽

THE first compilation of the famous prayers of the renowned mystics and adepts of all ages.

The book *Mystics at Prayer* explains in simple language the reason for prayer, how to pray, and the Cosmic laws involved. You come to learn the real efficacy of prayer and its full beauty dawns upon you. Whatever your religious beliefs, this book makes your prayers the application not of words, but of helpful, divine principles. You will learn the infinite power of prayer. Prayer is man's rightful heritage. It is the direct means of man's communion with the infinite force of divinity.

Mystics at Prayer is well bound, printed on art paper in two colors, with deckle-edged pages, sent anywhere, postpaid, $1.70 (12/9 sterling).

VOLUME X
Behold the Sign
By RALPH M. LEWIS, F.R.C.

▽

WHAT were the *Sacred Traditions* said to have been revealed to Moses—and never spoken by the ancient Hebrews? What were the forces of nature discovered by the Egyptian priesthood and embodied in strange symbols—symbols which became the ever-living knowledge which built King Solomon's Temple, and which found their way into the secret teachings of every century?

Regardless of the changing consciousness of man, certain signs and devices have immortalized for all ages the truths which make men free. Learn the meaning of the Anchor and Ark, the Seven-Pointed Star, ancient Egyptian hieroglyphs, and *many other age-old secret symbols.*

Here is a book that also explains the origin of the various forms of the cross, the meanings of which are often misunderstood. It further points out the mystical beginnings of the *secret signs* used by many fraternal orders today. This book of symbolism is *fully illustrated*, simply and interestingly written. Well bound and printed. Price, postage prepaid, $1.60 (11/9 sterling).

VOLUME XI

Mansions of the Soul

THE COSMIC CONCEPTION

By H. SPENCER LEWIS, F.R.C., Ph.D.

▽

REINCARNATION! The world's most disputed doctrine. The belief in reincarnation has had millions of intelligent, learned, and tolerant followers throughout the ages. Ringing through the minds and hearts of students, mystics, and thinkers have always been the words: "Why Are We Here?" Reincarnation has been criticized by some as conflicting with sacred literature and as being without verification. This book reveals, however, in an intelligent manner the many facts to support reincarnation. Quotations from eminent authorities, and from Biblical and Sacred works substantiate reincarnation. This volume PROVES reincarnation. It places it high above mere speculation. This book is without exaggeration the most complete, inspiring, enlightening book ever written on this subject. It is not a fiction story but a step-by-step revelation of profound mystical laws. Look at *some* of these thought-provoking, intriguing subjects:

The Cosmic Conception; The Personality of the Soul; Does Personality Survive Transition?; Heredity and Inheritance; Karma and Personal Evolution; Religious and Biblical Viewpoints; Christian References; Between Incarnations; Souls of Animals and the "Unborn"; Recollections of the Past.

The book contains over three hundred pages. Beautifully printed, neatly bound, stamped in gold, it will be a valuable asset to your library. Economically priced at only $3.00 (£1/2/- sterling) per copy, postage prepaid.

VOLUME XII

Lemuria—The Lost Continent of the Pacific

By Wishar S. Cerve

▽

BENEATH the rolling, restless seas lie the mysteries of forgotten civilizations. Swept by the tides, half-buried in the sands, worn away by terrific pressure, are the remnants of a culture little known to our age of today. Where the mighty Pacific now rolls in a majestic sweep of thousands of miles, there was once a vast continent. This land was known as Lemuria, and its people as Lemurians.

We pride ourselves upon the inventions, conveniences, and developments of today. We call them modern, but these ancient and long-forgotten people excelled us. Things we speak of as future possibilities, they knew as everyday realities. Science has gradually pieced together the evidences of this lost race, and in this book you will find the most amazing, enthralling revelations you have ever read. How these people came to be swept from the face of the earth, except for survivors who have living descendants today, is explained. Illustrations and explanations of their mystic symbols, maps of the continent, and many ancient truths and laws are contained in this unusual book.

If you are a lover of mystery, of the unknown, the weird— read this book. Remember, however, this book *is not fiction*, but based on facts, the result of extensive research. Does civilization reach a certain height and then retrograde? Are the culture and progress of mankind in cycles, reaching certain peaks, and then returning to start over again? These questions and many more are answered in this intriguing volume. Read of the living descendants of these people, whose expansive nation now lies at the bottom of the Pacific. In the minds of these descendants is the knowledge of the principles which in bygone centuries made their forebears builders of an astounding civilization.

The book, *Lemuria—The Lost Continent of the Pacific,* is beautifully bound, well printed, and contains many illustrations. It is economically priced at $2.95 (£1/1/9 sterling), postpaid.

VOLUME XIII
The Technique of the Master
THE WAY OF COSMIC PREPARATION
By RAYMUND ANDREA, F.R.C.

▽

A GUIDE to inner unfoldment! The newest and simplest explanation for attaining the state of Cosmic Consciousness. To those who have felt the throb of a vital power within, and whose inner vision has at times glimpsed infinite peace and happiness, this book is offered. It converts the intangible whispers of self into forceful actions that bring real joys and accomplishments in life. It is a masterful work on psychic unfoldment.

It is well bound in cloth. Secure this treasure for yourself. Economically priced, postage prepaid, at $2.50 (18/3 sterling).

VOLUME XIV
The Symbolic Prophecy of
The Great Pyramid
By H. SPENCER LEWIS, F.R.C., Ph.D.

▽

THE world's greatest mystery and first wonder is the Great Pyramid. It stands as a monument to the learning and achievements of the ancients. For centuries its secrets were closeted in stone—now they stand revealed.

Never before in a book priced within the reach of every reader have the history, vast wisdom, and prophecies of the Great Pyramid been given. You will be amazed at the Pyramid's scientific construction and at the tremendous knowledge of its mysterious builders.

Who built the Great Pyramid? Why were its builders inspired to reveal to posterity the events of the future? What is the path that the Great Pyramid indicates lies before mankind? Within the pages of this enlightening book are the answers to many enthralling questions. It prophesied the World Wars and the great economic upheaval. Learn what it presages for the future. You must not deprive yourself of this book.

The book is well bound with a cloth cover, and contains instructive charts and illustrations. Priced at only $2.75 (£1/-/- sterling) with postage paid.

VOLUME XV

The Book of Jasher

THE SACRED BOOK WITHHELD

▽

BY WHAT right has man been denied the words of the prophets? Who dared expunge from the Holy Bible one of its inspired messages? For centuries man has labored under the illusion that there have been preserved for him the collected books of the great teachers and disciples—yet one has been withheld—*The Book of Jasher*.

Within the hallowed pages of the great Bible itself are references to this lost book which have puzzled the devout and students for centuries. As if by Divine decree, the Bible appears to cry out to mankind that its sanctity has been violated, its truth veiled, for we find these two passages exclaiming: "Is not this written in the Book of Jasher?"—Joshua 10:13; "Behold, it is written in the Book of Jasher"—2 Samuel 1:18.

Alcuin discovered this great book of the Bible written by Jasher. He translated it from the Hebrew in 800 A.D. Later it was suppressed and then rediscovered in 1829, and once again suppressed.

But now we bring to you an actual photographic reproduction of this magnificent work, page for page, line for line, unexpurgated. This enlightening work, bound in its original style, is priced at only $2.95 (£1/1/9 sterling) per copy, postage paid.

VOLUME XVI

The Technique of the Disciple

By RAYMUND ANDREA, F.R.C.

▽

The Technique of the Disciple is a book containing a modern description of the ancient esoteric path to spiritual illumination, trod by the masters and avatars of yore. It has long been said that Christ left, as a great heritage to members of His secret council, a private method for guidance in life, which method has been preserved until today in the secret, occult, mystery schools.

Raymund Andrea, the author, reveals the method for attaining a greater life taught in these mystery schools, which perhaps parallels the secret instructions of Christ to members of His council. The book is enlightening, inspiring, and splendidly written. It is handsomely bound with a stiff board cover and the material of the cover is woven of silk thread, and stamped in gold. Postage prepaid. Priced at $2.50 (18/3 sterling).

VOLUME XVIII
Glands—Our Invisible Guardians
By M. W. KAPP, M.D.

▽

You need not continue to be bound by those glandular characteristics of your life which do not please you. These influences, through the findings of science and the mystical principles of nature, may be adjusted. The first essential is that of the old adage: "Know Yourself." Have revealed the facts about the endocrine glands—know where they are located in your body and what mental and physical functions they control. The control of the glands can mean the control of your life. These facts, scientifically correct, with their mystical interpretation, are for the first time presented in simple, nontechnical language, in a book which everyone can enjoy and profit by reading.

Mystics and metaphysicians have long recognized that certain influences and powers of a Cosmic nature could be tapped; that a Divine energy could be drawn upon, which affects our creative ability, our personality, and our physical welfare. For centuries there has been speculation as to what area or what organs of the body contain this medium—this contact between the Divine and the physical. Now it is known that certain of the glands are governors which speed up or slow down the influx of Cosmic energy into the body. What this process of Divine alchemy is and how it works is fascinatingly explained in this book of startling facts.

Dr. M. W. Kapp, the author, during his lifetime was held in high esteem by the medical fraternity despite the fact that he also expressed a deep insight into the mystical laws of life and their influence on the physical functioning of the body.

INTRODUCTION BY H. SPENCER LEWIS, F.R.C., Ph.D.

Dr. H. Spencer Lewis—first Imperator of the Rosicrucian Order (AMORC), of North and South America, for its present cycle of activity, and author of many works on mysticism, philosophy, and metaphysics—wrote an important introduction to this book, in which he highly praised it and its author.

The book is well bound with a cloth cover; price only $1.95 (14/6 sterling) with postage paid.

VOLUME XXI

What to Eat—And When

By STANLEY K. CLARK, M.D., C.M., F.R.C.

▽

"MIND over matter" is not a trite phrase. Your moods, your temperament, your very *thoughts* can and *do* affect digestion. Are you overweight—or underweight? Appearances, even the scales, are not always reliable. Your age, your sex, the kind of work you do—all these factors determine whether your weight is correct or wrong for *you*. Do you know that some people suffer from food allergy? Learn these interesting facts, and how your digestion may be affected even hours after you have eaten.

The author of this book, Dr. Stanley K. Clark, was for several years staff physician at the Henry Ford Hospital in Detroit. He is a noted gastroenterologist (specialist in stomach and intestinal disorders). He brings you his wealth of knowledge in this field, *plus* his additional findings from his study of the effects of the *mind* upon digestion.

What to Eat—And When is compact, free from unnecessary technical terminology. Includes complete handy index, *food chart*, and *sample menus*. It is not a one-time-reading book. You will often refer to it throughout the years. Well printed, strongly bound. Price, postpaid to you, $2.20 (16/– sterling).

VOLUME XXII
The Sanctuary of Self
By RALPH M. LEWIS, F.R.C.

▽

WHAT could be more essential than the discovery and analysis of *self*, the composite of that consciousness which constitutes one's whole being? This book of sound logic presents revealingly and in entirety the four phases of human living: The Mysteries, The Technique, The Pitfalls, and Attainment.

Do you not, at times, entertain the question as to whether you are living your life to your best advantage? You may find an answer in some of the 23 chapters, presented under headings such as: Causality and Karma, The Lost Word, Death—The Law of Change, Love and Desire, Nature of Dreams, Prediction, Mastership and Perfection. Consider "Love and Desire." In much of ancient and modern literature, as well as in the many and various preachments of the present-day world, LOVE is proclaimed as the solution to all human conflict. Do you understand truly the meaning of *absolute love?* Do you know that there are various *loves* and that some of the so-called loves are dangerous drives?

Written authoritatively by Ralph M. Lewis, Imperator of the Rosicrucian Order (AMORC), the international jurisdiction of North, Central, and South America, British Commonwealth and Empire, France, Switzerland, Sweden, and Africa, this volume of over 350 pages, carefully indexed, is of particular value as a text for teachers and students of metaphysics, including philosophy and psychology. Well-bound and attractive, it is purposely economically priced at $3.10 (£1/2/9 sterling), postpaid, making it available to all sincere seekers.

VOLUME XXIII

Sepher Yezirah—A Book on Creation

OR THE JEWISH METAPHYSICS OF
REMOTE ANTIQUITY

DR. ISIDOR KALISCH, Translator

▽

AMONG the list of the hundred best books in the world, one
might easily include this simple volume, revealing the greatest
authentic study of the secret Kabala.

The *Sepher Yezirah* has 61 pages with both Hebrew and
English texts, photolithographed from the 1877 original edition.

The careful reader will be attracted to three characteristics
of this edition:

(1) A clear English translation of a most ancient work, almost unavailable up to the present.
(2) A simple exposé of fundamental aspects of the ancient
Kabala without superstitious interpretations.
(3) An inexpensive and convenient translation of the world's
oldest philosophical writing in Hebrew.

Attractive and convenient, paper-bound edition. Price postpaid, $1.40 (10/3 sterling).

VOLUME XXIV

Of Gods and Miracles

WONDROUS TALES OF THE ANCIENT EGYPTIANS

By Ulrich Steindorff Carrington

▽

Over fifty centuries ago in the land of the Nile, man gained his first insight into spiritual values—long before any of the living religions or great philosophies began, these truths were incorporated in simple tales. Fathers related them to their sons. Sages told their disciples.

These stories are not a modern historian's version of ancient times. No one speaks for these sages. They speak for themselves—you will read words written 2000 years before Christ! Great truths between the lines concerning the simple characters and incidents will stand revealed. They are as effective today as when first inscribed in stone or written upon papyrus scrolls.

Here we have authentic works translated by world-recognized Egyptologists. Ulrich Steindorff Carrington, the author, is son of the late Dr. George Steindorff, world-famous Egyptologist and former consultant for the Rosicrucian Museum. Postpaid, only $2.75 (£1/-/- sterling).

VOLUME XXV

Son of the Sun

By SAVITRI DEVI

▽

THE amazing story of Akhnaton (Amenhotep IV), Pharaoh of Egypt 1360 B.C. This is not just the fascinating story of a man's life—it is far more. It raises the curtain on man's emerging from superstition and idolatry. Against the tremendous opposition of a fanatical and politically corrupt priesthood, Akhnaton brought about the world's first spiritual revolution. He was the first to declare a "sole God." In the words of Sir Flinders Petrie (*History of Egypt*): "Were it invented to satisfy our modern scientific conceptions, his religio-philosophy could not be logically improved upon at the present day."

This book, of 322 pages, will be shipped to you direct from London, England. It is priced most economically at $2.95 (£1/1/9 sterling), postpaid.

VOLUME XXVI

The Conscious Interlude

By Ralph M. Lewis, F.R.C.

▽

How many of the countless subjects which shape your life are inherited ideas? How many are actually yours? Would you like to have your own mind look at itself in perspective for an analysis? In this book, Mr. Lewis, Imperator of the international Rosicrucian Order, AMORC, outlines the culmination of years of his original thought. As you follow him through the pages into broad universal concepts, your mind too will feel its release into an expanding consciousness.

You will answer such questions as: Is consciousness something innate or is it generated? What are your own conscious interludes? This work belongs to every seeker after knowledge.

Indexed and illustrated, a volume of more than 360 pages, priced at only $3.75 (£1/7/3 sterling), postpaid.